First Facts™

Learning about Money

What Do Banks Do?

by Roberta Basel

Consultant:
Sharon M. Danes, PhD
Professor and Family Economist
University of Minnesota

Capstone
press
Mankato, Minnesota

First Facts is published by Capstone Press,
151 Good Counsel Drive, P.O. Box 669, Mankato, Minnesota 56002.
www.capstonepress.com

Library of Congress Cataloging-in-Publication Data
Basel, Roberta.
    What do banks do? / by Roberta Basel.
    p. cm. — (First facts. Learning about money)
    Summary: "Introduces how banks help people handle money, including checking and
savings accounts, loans, and other services"—Provided by publisher.
    Includes bibliographical references and index.
    ISBN-13: 978-0-7368-5398-9 (hardcover)
    ISBN-10: 0-7368-5398-7 (hardcover)
    1. Banks and banking—Juvenile literature. I. Title. II. Series.
HG1609.B37 2006
332.1'7—dc22   2005020619

Editorial Credits
Wendy Dieker, editor; Jennifer Bergstrom, set designer; Bobbi J. Dey, book designer;
    Jo Miller, photo researcher/photo editor

Photo Credits
Art Directors/Spencer Grant, 6
Capstone Press/Karon Dubke, cover, 5, 7, 8–9, 10, 13, 14–15, 17, 21
Corbis/Michael Keller, 19
SuperStock/Mark Udry, 18
Young Americans Center for Financial Education, 20

1 2 3 4 5 6 11 10 09 08 07 06

Table of Contents

Going to the Bank

   The Smiths are going to the bank. Mrs. Smith needs money to buy a car. Evan wants to put cash in his savings account. Tess has a piggy bank full of coins, and she'd like dollar bills instead.

   A bank is a business that does all of these things. Banks help people take care of their money.

Fun Fact!
Pennsylvania Bank was the first bank in the United States. It opened in 1780.

Keeping Money Safe

Banks keep money safe. They have **vaults** with heavy doors and strong locks. Vaults also have boxes where customers can keep valuable things.

At the bank, people **deposit**, or put, money in accounts. An account is a record of your **balance**. You can put in and take out money when you need to.

Checking Accounts

Mrs. Smith puts money in a checking account so she can use it later. She writes checks at stores to pay for things. Then the bank gives the stores money from Mrs. Smith's account.

Customers get checks from the bank. Mrs. Smith orders blue checks.

Fun Fact!
Many banks also offer debit cards. Debit cards are small plastic cards that work just like checks.

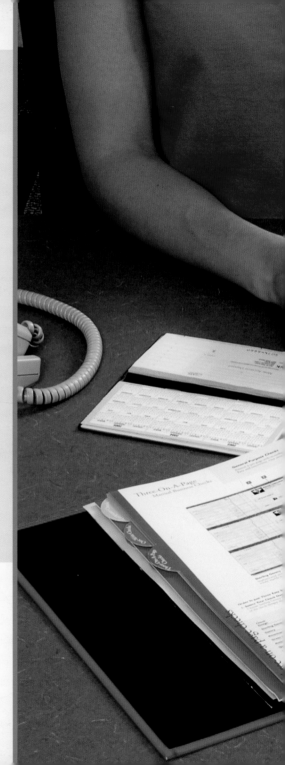

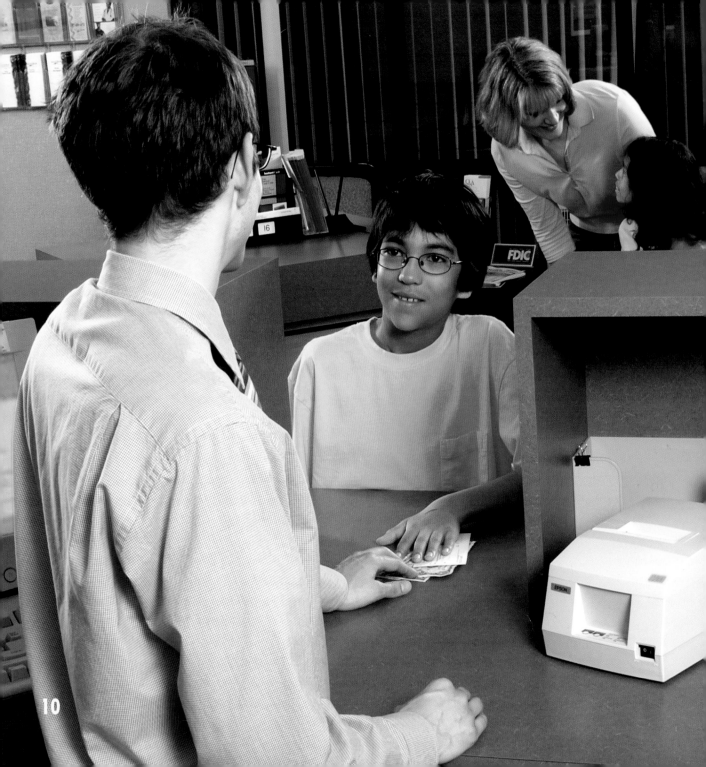

Savings Accounts

Savings accounts are for keeping money for a long time. Evan is saving for college. He deposits cash today. Evan will take out, or **withdraw**, money when he needs to pay for college.

Banks pay people to keep money in savings accounts. This extra money is called **interest**. Each month, the bank adds extra money to Evan's account.

Fun Fact!
Little bits of money add up over time. If you deposit $2 a week, you will have over $100 at the end of a year!

Where Does My Cash Go?

The cash you deposit isn't kept for just you. Banks keep a record of the amount you deposit and then use the cash. Other customers get the cash when they need money. You won't get back the same bills and coins you deposit.

Tess exchanged her coins for bills. She got some of the cash Evan deposited.

Loans

Mrs. Smith needs money to buy a car. She doesn't have enough. The bank gives her a **loan** to buy the car. She will pay back the money a little at a time.

Banks charge people for loans. Mrs. Smith pays a little extra money, also called interest, each month.

Other Bank Services

Banks offer services to help their customers. People can cash checks or get money to spend in other countries. Some banks have machines for exchanging coins for paper money.

Just like stores, banks work to earn money. People usually have to pay for bank services.

Electronic Banking

Many banks offer electronic services that make banking easy. **ATMs** let people get cash from their accounts when the bank is closed.

Online banking lets customers check their accounts using home computers. As times change, banks will continue to offer new electronic banking services.

Amazing but True!

The Young Americans Bank in Denver, Colorado, is a bank just for kids. This bank teaches kids about money and banking. With an adult, kids can open checking and savings accounts through the mail. Kids from all over the world use this bank.

Hands On: Savings Account

You can learn with your family about how a savings account works. Your parents can be the bankers, and you can open a pretend savings account at home.

What You Need

notebook
pen or pencil
money to save

What You Do

1. "Deposit" some money. Give your "banker" the cash.
2. Draw three columns on the notebook page. Label them Date, Deposit or Withdraw, and Total.
3. Write the amount of the deposit in the Deposit or Withdraw column. For your first deposit, write the same amount in the Total column.
4. Each time you put in or take out money, write the amount in the Deposit or Withdraw column. Then add the deposits to the total. Subtract the withdrawals from the total. Write the new total in the column.

Remember that you can't withdraw more than the total. Try to deposit more than you withdraw. You will see your money grow!

Glossary

ATM (AYE-TEE-EM)—a machine that lets people get cash, make deposits, and move money between accounts; ATM stands for automated teller machine.

balance (BAL-uhns)—the amount of money in an account

deposit (di-POZ-it)—to put money into a bank account

interest (IN-trist)—the little extra money paid on balances; banks pay interest to savings accounts, and customers pay interest on loans.

loan (LOHN)—money borrowed from the bank

vault (VAWLT)—the room or container in a bank for keeping things safe

withdraw (with-DRAW)—to take money out of a bank account

Read More

Attebury, Nancy Garhan. *Out and About at the Bank.* Field Trips. Minneapolis: Picture Window Books, 2006.

Hall, Margaret. *Banks.* Earning, Saving, Spending. Chicago: Heinemann Library, 2000.

Johnston, Marianne. *Let's Visit the Bank.* Our Community. New York: PowerKids Press, 2000.

Internet Sites

FactHound offers a safe, fun way to find Internet sites related to this book. All of the sites on FactHound have been researched by our staff.

Here's how:
1. Visit *www.facthound.com*
2. Type in this special code **0736853987** for age-appropriate sites. Or enter a search word related to this book for a more general search.
3. Click on the **Fetch It** button.

FactHound will fetch the best sites for you!

Index